WHAT THE SKY ARRANGES

WHAT THE SKY ARRANGES

Poems made from the

TSUREZUREGUSA of KENKŌ

by

ANDREW FITZSIMONS

with drawings by
Sergio Maria Calatroni

ISOBAR
PRESS

First published in 2014 by

Isobar Press
Sakura 2-21-23-202
Setagaya-ku
Tokyo 156-0053
Japan

http://isobarpress.com

ISBN 978-4-907359-02-7

ACKNOWLEDGEMENTS

Acknowledgements are due to the editors of the following
publications in which some of these poems first appeared: *The
Dublin Review, Fortnight,* and *Stand.* A selection of these poems
appeared in the online anthology *Emerging from Absence: An
Archive of Japan in English-Language Verse,* and in the anthology
Our Shared Japan (Dedalus Press, 2007).

I am indebted to Donald Keene's translation, *Essays in
Idleness: The Tsurezuregusa of Kenkō* (New York: Columbia
University Press, 1967), and G.B. Sansom's translation *Kenkō:
Essays in Idleness* (1911).

CONTENTS

for Sheena and Joe

AFTERWARDS

Headspinning to realise
I've been sitting here for days
this pen in hand
these thoughts to mind

THE EXILE'S MOON

So quietly in the house
no-one could know whether in or out.
How much worse to have to face
conversation on an empty heart.
I could almost envy Ovid his *Tristia*;
that full moon over the Black Sea.

THE HOLY MAN OF KUME

What tools men are!
Led by dong and nose.
The scent that clings to clothes
lasts no longer
than a flea, and yet
should a whiff come near
the heart fails to beat.
Example (from legend):
holy man with magic power
catches glimpse of girl
bathing in river.
Swoons. Loses gift of flight.
Understandable, I suppose.
Her arms, her flesh, her smile.

KUROKAMI

Some woman's raven hair
has maddened every mother's son.
Her first words uttered,
hidden behind a screen
reveal her future flavour.
Our love is rooted
in the deepest, darkest place;
the Empire of the Senses
we should resist without disgrace.
One ache, infatuation, rises
beyond all other whims – in young
in old, in the foolish and the wise.
You could fetter an elephant,
they say, with a rope of woman's hair,
and with a sandal worn by woman
make a flute to summon deer.
O the senses leave you maddened,
avoid her raven hair.

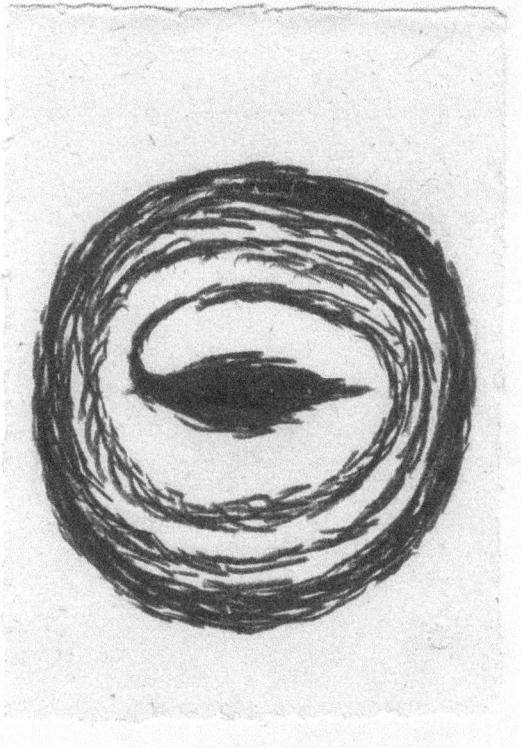

READING

To sit under the lamp alone
a book spread out before you:
bliss. The past unfolds,
on fire with life. Lao Tzu
I read, the sage Chuang Tzu,
whose dream I dream as darkness falls.

WORLDS

Travel. Wherever you go
the world you bring with you
is washed by the world you see.

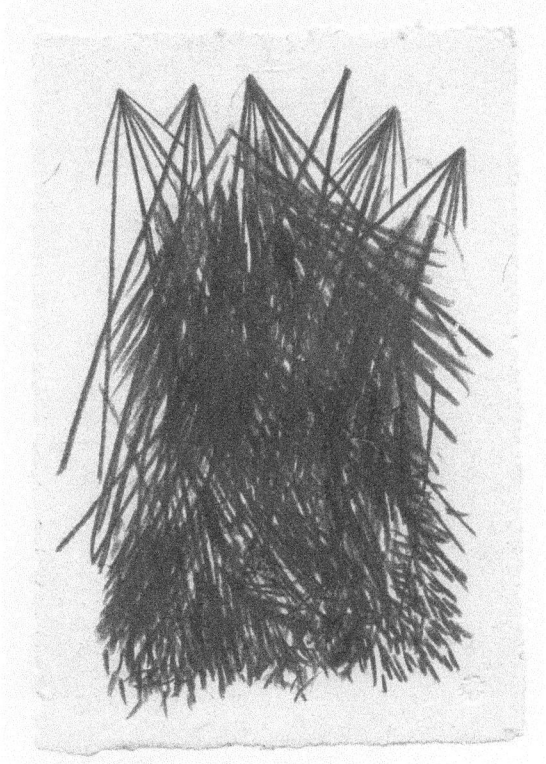

MUSICS

The Kagura dance is captivating,
to the sound of reed pipe and flute;
though I incline most to the watery mood
that spills through me when fingertip meets string.

THE HERMIT

A man who had nothing once said:
'One thing even I
would be loth to see go:
the beauty of a winter sky.'
And now we know why.

THE HEART

The moon never disappoints.
Nor dew.
Wind sufflates the hollow heart.
The clear stream pores over rocks.
The heart exhales mountains and lakes,
birds and fish.

WHAT'S WHAT

Why bother with the bad?
Why, knowing what's what,
waste time with criticism?
And what about the idiots
who go on about Art
and know next-to-nothing about it?

THE RISEN TIDE

Impermanent is the risen tide.
Yesterday's pools, tomorrow's puddles.
Exeunt omnes. Tempus fugit.

What does day teach the day?
The peach and damson trees
in the garden will not say.

X

The days and the months and the years
scattered like a loose bloom
before even a breeze blew near.
What you said and what you did
still run through me like delirium,
though we're as close now as the dead.

THE AUTUMN NIGHT

I pass the long autumn nights
tearing up old notes and letters,
putting the afterlife in order;
word by word,
self upon dishevelled self remembered.
And then I light upon
a dead friend's thoughts
and somewhere a high door opens
and I am silent, stared at,
by night, by dawn.

A LETTER

On a morning of snow I wrote a letter.
'And how could you write and not mention the snow?'
Dear friend, long departed, it is snowing again.

NAMES

And some there are just ask for it.
Like that old crank lived
by a giant nettle
so was nicknamed *Mr Prickly,*
cut it down became *Stumpy,*
dug that up was called *Mole.*

DATES

Don't wait till dotage for your goodness to begin.
Look at the dates on those gravestones.

ORNAMENTS

What is bad taste?
too many knick-knacks about the place
too many brushes in the ink-box
too many Buddhas
too many shrubs and plants in a garden
too many rooms in a house
too many words on meeting someone
a ledger all plus and no minus?

THE AIR

Intolerable: every wind that blows
carries news of another scandal,
and here's this one knows every detail,
spreads the word like a death in the family;
stop up your ears it will still filter through,
like the words of a song never listened to.

FIRE

Insufferable: fad gadgets,
their acolytes;
at prayer, in code;
leaving the rest of us out.
The one I admire?
This what-they-call neophyte
only now finding use for fire.

A CURSE

When they were levelling the ground to build
the new City Offices, workmen came upon a mound
where images of snakes and coiled creatures lay buried.
These are the gods of the people of the place as it was before,
they said, what should we do? Some on the Council argued:
These things have been here since ancient times, it would be wrong
to root them up and build over them. Then the Chief Minister spoke:
What curse could these creatures place upon our new dispensation?
These ancients have no power over us now. Away with such images.
The workmen destroyed the mound and the coils went into museums.
Maybe the Minister was right. Though who today would recognize a curse?

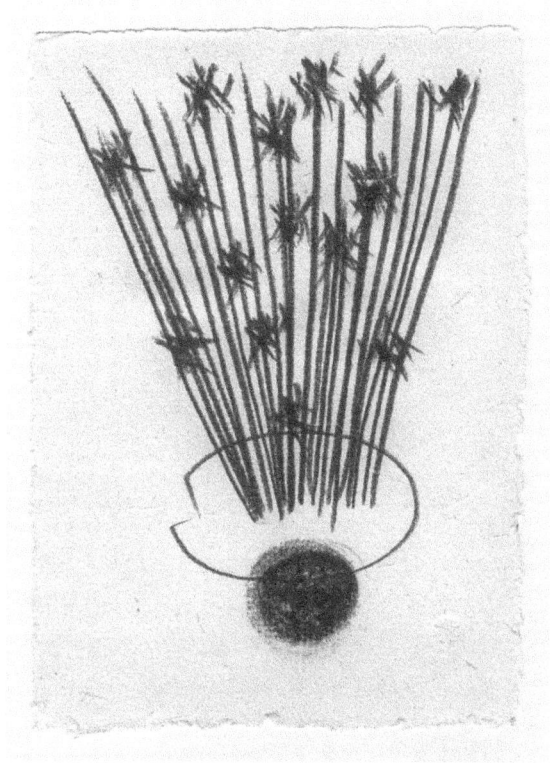

A GARDEN

Trees. Pine and cherry.
Five-needled pine.
Cherry: with single flowers.
Never the double:
the Kanzan's dense clusters,
the countless petals
of a Cheal's Weeping.
Plum blossoms: white and pink.
The early-blooming single,
the scented double crimson.
Late plum shrinks
under a cherry din.
Willows convince.
Maple leaves turn on
and off in season.
Orange trees and laurels
when the trunks are old and big.
Plants: kerria roses,
wisteria, irises and pinks.
For a pond, water lilies of course.
In autumn, reeds, pampas grass,
bellflowers, bush clover,
asters, burnet, gentians,
chrysanthemums (the yellow ones).
Ivy, arrowroot vine, morning
glories on a low fence,
not too high, and not too many.

GAME THEORY

What a boardgame teaches:
never play to win, play not to lose.
Know what moves will be soonest defeated,
delay your fate, if only by a single throw of the dice.

FRIENDS

Seven types make bad friends:
the powerful; the young; the never-sick-a-day;
the lush; the soldier;
the liar; the skinflint.
Three friends you would want:
A gift-giver; a doctor;
a friend who is wise.

MORE ADVICE

Have nothing to leave when you die. Why?
Gewgaws, holy trinkets, will mock you when you're gone;
much-loved bric-a-brac becomes a grief each day
for the ones we love who love us in return.
So? Divvy up now not later.
Despise, disdain the tilth of your years.
Better to pass and have not left a trace.
Best not to have been here in the first place.

THE CLASSICS

Quinqueremes and galleons:
ivory, apes, peacocks
sandalwood, cedarwood, sweet white wine;
diamonds, emeralds, amethysts
topazes, cinnamon, gold moidores.
Then there are books that say
do not prize what comes from afar,
set no store by the hard to obtain.

MIRROR

How to know we do not please the eye?
How to know in our hearts we are fools?
How to know that we have no talent?
How to know we do not count for much?
How to know we've grown old with the years?
How to know that sickness has bitten?
How to know how close death's touch is?
How to know how true we have been?
Can we know our own lies, our own lives?
Can we know the lies and lives of others?

You say you can look in a mirror,
You can tell someone's age by the years,
That the heart of man is knowable.
Then shouldn't your life now change?

THE HUMAN

This business of life, getting on –
like making a snowman in Spring:
scrimshawed stones, brassoed buttons,
that touch of the human,
and a soundless dripping within.

NIGHT

Night deepens the world's beauty:
a lamplit face glows against ebony;
and from a voice in the dark
that trace – knowing someone might hear –
moves beyond the clamour of plain day.

HOLY GROUND

On days no-one else goes
go to holy ground, by night.

WHAT THE SKY ARRANGES

The autumn moon is beautiful. Nothing compares.
You with no time for what the sky arranges,
look, the moon waxes, wanes, always changes.

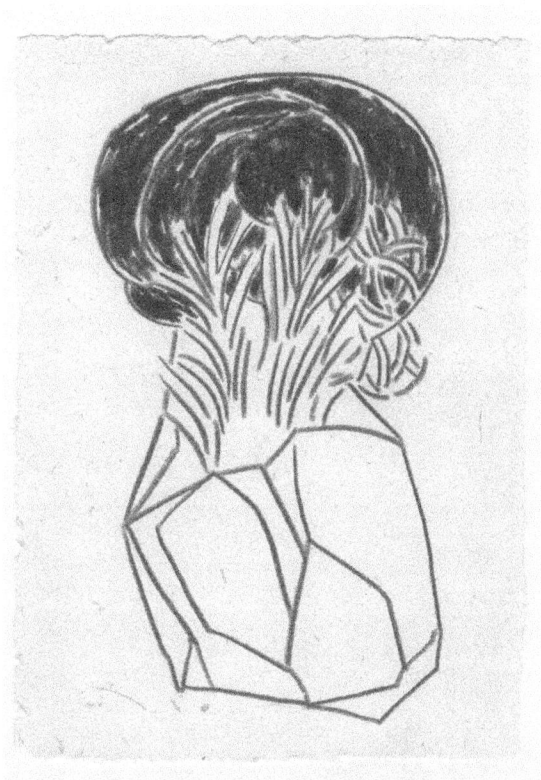

www.ingramcontent.com/pod-product-compliance
Lightning Source LLC
Chambersburg PA
CBHW031217090426
42736CB00009B/957